## A ROOKIE BIOGRAPHY

# *BENJAMIN FRANKLIN*

## *A Man with Many Jobs*

By Carol Greene

 CHILDRENS PRESS®

CHICAGO

*This book is for Dennis and Carole.*

**Benjamin Franklin**

LIBRARY OF CONGRESS
Library of Congress Cataloging-in-Publication Data

Greene, Carol.
    Benjamin Franklin : a man with many jobs / by Carol
Greene ; Steve Dobson, illustrator.
        p.   cm. — (A Rookie biography)
    Summary: Traces the life and accomplishments of the
printer, philosopher, scientist, inventor, and statesman.
    ISBN 0-516-04202-5
    1. Franklin, Benjamin, 1706-1790—Juvenile literature.
2. Statesmen—United States—Biography—Juvenile literature.
[1. Franklin, Benjamin, 1706-1790. 2. Statesmen.]
I. Dobson, Steve, ill. II. Title. III. Series: Greene, Carol. Rookie
biography.
E302.6.F8G797   1988
973.3'092'4—dc19
[92]                                                        88-15011
                                                              CIP
Childrens Press®, Chicago                        AC

  11 12 13 14 15 16 17 18 19 R 02 01 00 99

Benjamin Franklin
was a real person.
He lived from 1706 to 1790.
Some exciting things happened
during his life.
He saw many of them.
He even helped
some of them happen.
This is his story.

## TABLE OF CONTENTS

Benjamin Franklin's mother

An artist drew this picture
of Josiah and Abiah Franklin
with their children.

The Franklin
family lived in
this house
in Boston,
Massachusetts.

# Chapter 1

# Benjamin Says No

Back in 1713,
fathers picked the jobs
their children would do.

"You will learn
to be a preacher,"
Mr. Franklin told his son.

"Yes, Father," said Benjamin.

He went to a special
school in Boston.
He did very well.

But after a year,
Mr. Franklin changed his mind.
"Preachers are poor," he said.
"You will go to a new school."

"Yes, Father," said Benjamin.

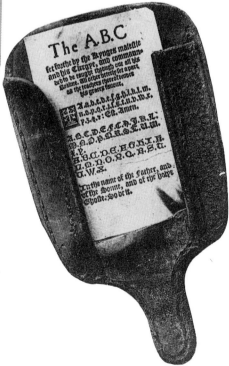

Children learned
from horn books.
The book shown
above was made
of slate. The book
shown at right
held lessons
written on paper.

Some children went to school. Most children
were taught reading, writing, and arithmetic at home.

He went to the new school.

He learned to write well.

But he failed arithmetic.

Two years went by.
"You are ten now,"
said Mr. Franklin.
"You will quit school
and work for me."

"Yes, Father," said Benjamin.

Mr. Franklin made
soap and candles.
It was hard, smelly work.
Benjamin did not like it.
But he did it
for two years.

This painting of a candle shop shows how candles were made.

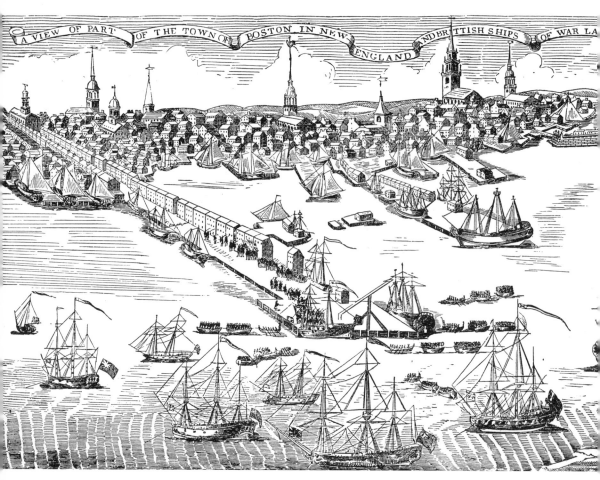

Boston was a big city. Many ships sailed in and out of its harbor.

Then one day Benjamin said,
"I want to go to sea."

"No," said Mr. Franklin.
"Your brother drowned at sea.
You will stay in Boston."

"Yes, Father," said Benjamin.

They looked at other jobs.
"You can lay bricks
or work with metal,"
said Mr. Franklin.
"You can be an apprentice."

Benjamin thought.
Apprentices had to work hard
for just one person.
They were not free
until they were 21.

"No, Father," said Benjamin.

# Chapter 2

# A Lot to Learn

"You must do *something*,"
said Mr. Franklin.
"I know!
You will be an apprentice
to your brother James.
That won't be so bad."

In the early days of printing, type was set by hand.

So Benjamin went to work
in James's printing shop.
He learned about printing.
Then he got bored.
"I must learn
other things too," he thought.

When he was older, Benjamin sold his poems.

So he practiced writing
and wrote some poems.
He worked on arithmetic
until he was good at it.

He practiced swimming
and did fancy tricks.

Once he lay on his back
and let a kite
pull him across a pond.

Most of all, he read
all the books he could find.
He even stopped eating meat
so he could buy more books.

But he still hated
being an apprentice.
James made him
do boring jobs.
Sometimes he beat Benjamin.

"This is no good,"
thought Benjamin
when he was 17.
"I have had enough.
I will run away."

# Chapter 3

# A Busy Man

Benjamin ran away
to Philadelphia, Pennsylvania.
For a while,
he worked for a printer.
Then he started
his own printing shop.

Benjamin worked hard
to make his printing
shop a success.

Deborah
Read

Soon he owned a newspaper
and a store too.
People liked him.
He made many friends.
In 1730,
he married Deborah Read.

Benjamin once printed on the wooden
printing press shown at left. Years later, an artist
painted Benjamin Franklin as a fireman.

Benjamin was busy now.
But he wanted to do more.
He started a library
and a fire department.
He wrote about science
and did experiments.

Franklin
invented a
new kind of stove.

He invented a chair
that turned into a ladder.
He invented a stove
that gave lots of heat.
Soon everyone wanted
a Franklin stove.

Then Benjamin wrote a book.
It told about farming
and weather and holidays.
He made up sayings
to put in it too.

"A penny saved
is a penny earned."
"Eat to live,
not live to eat."
"Fish and visitors
stink in three days."

What do you think of
Benjamin's sayings? Do you
think they make sense?

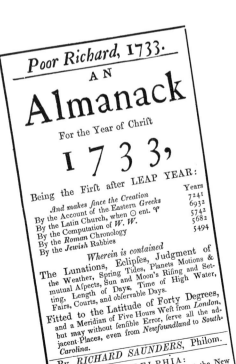

Benjamin called the book
*Poor Richard's Almanack.*
People loved it.
He wrote a new one
every year for 25 years.

Benjamin started a family too.
He had three children:
William, Francis, and Sarah.

When Francis was four,
he had a bad case of flu.
So Benjamin didn't make him
get a smallpox shot.
Then Francis caught smallpox
and died.

Benjamin felt terrible.
He wrote an article
so other parents
would get smallpox shots
for their children.

He thought about
little Francis often.
But he knew
what he had to do.
He had to keep busy.

Chapter 4

# Bright Ideas

Ideas buzzed like bees
in Benjamin's head.

"How can I become
a better person?"
he wondered.
"I know!"
He made up 13 rules.

"Don't eat or drink
too much," said one.
"Don't waste anything,"
said another.
"Don't hurt anyone,"
said a third.

Benjamin worked on
one rule each week.
Then he went on
to the next rule.
He started over after 13 weeks.

Benjamin liked to do experiments and show them to his friends.

Benjamin had ideas
about science too.
Many people played games
with electricity.

They made sparks
shoot from wires
or cakes of ice.
Sometimes they gave
other people shocks.

Benjamin liked the games.
But his idea
was not a game.
He thought that
electricity and lightning
were the same thing.

He also knew how to prove
his idea was right.

"Put a big box on top
of a high tower," he said.
"Put an iron rod in the box.
Have a man stand
in the box during a storm."

Some scientists in Europe
tried this experiment.
Lightning struck the rod.
It *was* electricity!

Then Benjamin had
another idea.

He put a wire
at the tip of a kite.
He tied a key
at the end of the string.
Then he flew the kite
during a storm.

Benjamin wrote about his kite experiment. These pictures show you how three different artists painted this famous experiment. How are the pictures the same? How are they different?

That idea worked too.
Lightning struck the wire.
Benjamin felt the shock
through the key.
Yes, electricity and lightning
were the same thing.

All at once,
Benjamin was famous.
Scientists in England
gave him a medal.
Important people
called him Dr. Franklin.

But Benjamin wanted
his idea to help people.
So he invented
the lightning rod.

People put the rod
on a building.
Lightning struck the rod
and went down a wire
to the ground.
The building was safe.

Many of Benjamin's ideas
helped people.
He felt proud of his work.
But he still had
important things to do.

Lightning rods were put on houses.
Some women even wore hats with
lightning rods.

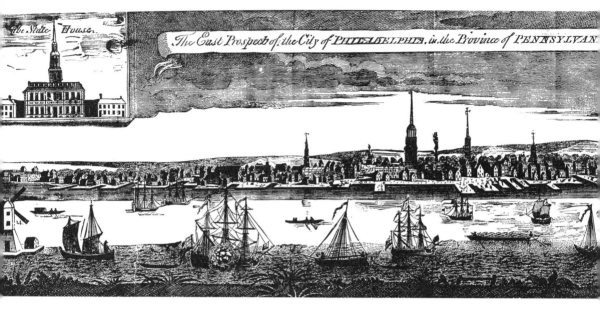

Philadelphia was a big city with brick buildings and brick streets. Benjamin Franklin lived and had his shop on High Street close to the Market Street Wharf.

# Chapter 5

# Benjamin and His Country

In those days,
England ruled America.
Pennsylvania was a colony,
not a state.

"Benjamin is a good talker,"
said people in Pennsylvania.
"He knows how to make
people do what he wants.
Let's send him to England.
He will help us there."

So Benjamin sailed to England.

He lived there for 16 years.

Then people in America said,

"We want to be free."

Rulers in England said, "No."

Benjamin Franklin tried to make the lawmakers in England
understand what the people in the thirteen colonies wanted.

Fighting broke out between the English soldiers and the colonists. Many people died.

Benjamin knew whose side
*he* was on.
He hurried home to America.
When he got there,
England and America
were at war.

Benjamin Franklin read and made some changes to
the Declaration of Independence written by Thomas Jefferson.

"We need you, Benjamin,"
said the American government.
So Benjamin worked
for the government.
He helped write the
Declaration of Independence.

Then the government
sent him to France.
"Ask the French people
to help us fight the English,"
they said.

In 1776 Franklin sailed to France to ask for help.

Benjamin was 70 years old.
He didn't feel well.
His clothes looked funny.
But he went to France.
The French people
loved him.

"We will help you," they said.
They did
and America won the war.

The king and queen of France listened to Benjamin Franklin and sent help.

Next, Benjamin helped
write the agreement
that ended the fighting.
Then he came home again.

Benjamin Franklin signed the peace treaty that ended
the war between England and America in Paris, France.

Benjamin Franklin was happy to be back in Philadelphia, Pennsylvania.

"We want you to be head
of the Pennsylvania government,"
said the people.
So he did that
for three years.

At last it was time
to write new rules
for the American government.
"Help us, Benjamin,"
said the people.
Benjamin did.

Working on the Constitution
of the United States
was Benjamin's last big job.
He wanted to do more.
He wanted to help
free the black slaves.
But he was old and tired.

Then he got sick
and had to stay in bed.
He read and wrote
as long as he could.
When he was 84,
Benjamin Franklin died.

Benjamin Franklin did many things in his life. Because
of his work on the Declaration of Independence (above left)
and the Constitution, his name will live forever.

He had done many jobs.
He had helped many people.
He had helped make
America free.

# Benjamin Franklin

1706 January 17—Born in Boston, Massachusetts to Josiah and Abiah Franklin

1718 Became apprentice to brother James

1723 Ran away to Philadelphia, Pennsylvania

1730 Married Deborah Read

1732 Wrote *Poor Richard's Almanack*

1747 Began work with electricity

1753 Invented lightning rod

1764 Went to England

1776 Signed Declaration of Independence
Went to France

1781 Worked on peace treaty

1787 Worked on Constitution

1790 April 17—Died in Philadelphia

# INDEX

**Page numbers in boldface type indicate illustrations.**

## PHOTO CREDITS

American Philosophical Society—39

Archives of 1776 © J.L.G. Ferris—18

Bettmann Archive—6, 7, 9, 12, 13, 14, 18, 19 (left), 20, 21, 23, 28, 29 (bottom), 32 (top), 34, 42, 44

CIGNA Museum—19 (right)

Historical Pictures Service, Chicago—4 (top left, bottom), 10, 15, 16, 17, 29 (top), 35, 36, 38, 40, 45

Historical Society of Pennsylvaina—32 (bottom), 42

Library Company of Philadelphia—25

North Wind Picture Archives—2, 31 (bottom), 45

Steve Dobson—Cover, 4 (top right), 27, 31 (top)

## ABOUT THE AUTHOR

Carol Greene has degrees in English Literature and Musicology. She has worked in international exchange programs, as an editor, and as a teacher. She now lives in St. Louis, Missouri, and writes full time. She has published over seventy books, most of them for children. Other Childrens Press biographies by Ms. Greene include *Louisa May Alcott, Marie Curie, Thomas Alva Edison, Hans Christian Andersen, Marco Polo,* and *Wolfgang Amadeus Mozart* in the People of Distinction series, *Sandra Day O'Conner, Mother Teresa, Indira Nehru Gandhi, Diana, Princess of Wales, Desmond Tutu,* and *Elie Wiesel* in the Picture-Story Biography series, and *Pocahontas* in the Rookie Biographies.